I AM YOU
WE ARE ONE

I AM YOU
WE ARE ONE

A STEP BY STEP GUIDE ON
How to Connect & Channel
High Frequency Beings

Marco Antonio & Miguel Angel Peralta.
The StarSeed Twins

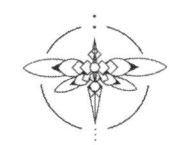

STARSEED TWINS

Connect in Social Media
IG: @StarSeed_Twins / @One_Who_Serves
YouTube: StarSeed Twins
Email: StarSeedTwins@gmail.com

This book is copyrighted material. All rights are reserved.
It is against the law to make copies of this material without getting specific written permission from SOMOS Publishing.
No part of this publication may be reproduced, stored in a retreival system, or transmitted in any form or by any means, electronic, mechanical, photocopying, recording, or otherwise, witout prior written permission of the publisher.

International rights and foreign translations are available only through.

SOMOS
PUBLISHING

Revised Edition 02- 2022

Dear divine ones,
Within, you possess everything you are
searching for on the outside.
Infinite love, infinite abundance, infinite wisdom;
It all belongs to you.
It is your divine right, and only you can give it all
to yourself.

StarSeed Twins

What's Inside

- Dedication
- About the Authors
- Introduction
- Meeting my Guides - The Pleiadians / Marco
- Meeting my Guides - Metatron / Miguel
- We are The Arcturians
- I AM YOU
- The Concept of Oneness
- You are not Alone
- The Polarity System
- You, Your Higher-Self & Higher Aspects
- Let the Message Come from Silence
- The Promise
- What is Channeling?
- What is Meditation?
- A Light Diet
- Creating a Sacred Space
- Tools & Objects
- The Power of Intention
- Trust Yourself
- Permission and self-validation
- Breathing Consciously
- Being present
- The Retrieved Information
- Observation, Non-Resistance & Fulfillment
- Questioning and Doubting
- The Process
- Connecting to your Heart
- The Meditation
- Commitment & Consistency
- Remembering the Warrior

Dedicated to YOU
We are ONE.

To the most incredible person who loved us unconditionally and wholeheartedly supported our lives, guiding us to become the best versions of ourselves: Our beloved mother, Maria de Los Angeles, "Mary of the Angels."

You have now become our principal Angel and Spirit Guide, watching over us with your unwavering love and guidance. We are forever grateful for the gift of life you gave us, and for being our beacon of love, compassion, and forgiveness.

Your legacy will live on in our hearts forever, and we will cherish the beautiful memories we created with you. Thank you for being our inspiration and for teaching us the true meaning of unconditional love.
We love you, Mom.

About the Authors
StarSeed Twins

Marco Antonio & Miguel Angel are true leaders in the ascension process and the new age higher consciousness movement. They are teachers of universal laws, leading and teaching by example, living and embodying Universal Truth, and practical application of this wisdom to everyday life.

Their profound connection to Source and the higher dimensional realms is unquestionable; it is palpable in the atmosphere when you are in their presence; it is a visceral experience.

Their energy signature alone acts as a catalyst to awakening and higher consciousness, even before they get to work with you one-on-one or in a group setting.

Marco and Miguel are clear channels for the highest loving guidance, which they download directly from Spirit. They will help you reconnect with your inner truth and readjust your trajectory in life, aligning you with your greater purpose.

They are naturally gifted, and their energy work is powerful and precise. The twins' intuitive senses and their ability to drop into complete surrender make them work with divine precision, like surgical master healers. It seems as if a divine source was wearing hand surgical gloves and using their bodies as a suit, for that is indeed what they are: Instruments of the Divine.

Working with them leads to accessing your own deepest and truest Source of power, mastery, and healing.

> We don't connect with Aliens; we connect with higher aspects of ourselves that have taught us how to fall in Love with our humanness.
> *Marco Antonio Peralta*

> Meditation is a practice of Self Love. It's the most honest moment where you will experience your authentic essence and where you'll learn unconditional Love toward yourself.
> *Miguel Angel Peralta*

Introduction
How it all started

We were born in a magical city in central Mexico called "Puebla of the Angels." Our mother was unaware she was giving birth to identical twins, and as a single parent, she had a tough time raising two boys on her own. She worked throughout the day to provide for our most basic necessities the best way she could. Still, the one thing she gave us abundantly was her unconditional love.

We will never forget when she looked us in the eye and told us, "You two are the best at anything you set your minds to." It was a simple phrase, but it stayed with us and became our life's mantra. We believed her; we had no reason to doubt her; after all, she was our mother, "humble, but rich in solid values." She was our rock, and with her struggles, she still managed to guide us through life's challenges.

Our upbringing was also shaped by our grandmother and aunts, who instilled in us a deep respect for life. Looking back, we realize how fortunate we were to have such strong and inspiring women around us. They taught us lessons that have stayed with us through the years, and we're forever grateful for their guidance and wisdom.

For many years, we carried a heavy burden in our hearts - the absence of our father. We went through life without ever having the chance to meet him, and this left us with a profound sense of bitterness and anger toward life and the divine. As a result, we sought refuge in vices like alcohol and cigarettes, leading us down a path of misbehavior and trouble.

My brother and I were filled with dreams and endless enthusiasm. However, we knew there was much to explore beyond our hometown. So at 14, we made the difficult decision to leave our beloved home and embark on a journey of self-discovery. Little did we know that this decision would change our lives forever. We decided to embark on incredible adventures as we navigated the obstacles by following our passions and finding our place in the world.

Despite our challenges, we held onto the hope that someday we would rise above our circumstances and become "the best versions of ourselves." Instead, throughout our teenage years, we moved to different cities with no real direction or sense of stability.

Finally, at 20, we migrated to the United Estates, hoping for a better life and opportunities. We adapted to the system, and our legal status at the time was not an excuse to grow in every aspect. So within a few months, we joined the university, got a job waiting tables, and made friends. Then, a few years later, we were offered to work for the most prominent financial institution in the country. We quickly moved up the ladder and became top producers in our field. At 27, we were at the top of our careers, growing financially, but still very lost in ourselves.

As time passed, we relocated to Miami after being terminated from our job for misconduct and failure to adhere to corporate protocols. We have again shattered, forced to start from scratch surrounded by disappointment. It took us a few years to recover and regain our footing as financial consultants. Initially, everything appeared to be going smoothly. Still, as we continued to ascend, we were met with a steep and inevitable decline. Then, in 2008, the Great Recession struck, and we lost everything again. The failure seemed interminable, and we were left feeling disoriented and overwhelmed, unsure of which path to take. Ultimately, we decided to take a break and start fresh.

Amid the turmoil, we began seeking growth by exploring our spiritual side. As we embarked on this journey, we became increasingly attuned to our innate ability to sense and connect with energy. Though we didn't initially dwell on it, we still tried to find meaning and direction in life. Yet, we eventually longed for a person absent from our lives; our father. So we took matters into our own hands and hired a detective to locate him.

So, it wasn't until we finally met him at age 37 that we started to understand who we were. We saw ourselves reflected in this man we had never known, and for the first time, we felt complete. But despite this feeling, we felt more empty than ever when he told us he couldn't be part of our lives, so we moved on. A series of events happened after we had closed this chapter, and new doors opened almost immediately, taking our paths in a new direction.

Shortly after emotionally and mentally detaching ourselves from the possibility of ever seeing our father again, our stepbrother "Emilio," our father's youngest son, called us. He told us everyone wanted to meet and bring us into their family. From that moment on, we formed a strong bond with this side of the family, whom we have grown to love deeply.

A transformative moment arrived when we turned 40. We felt a sudden urge to "awaken" and embark on a journey of self-exploration and deepen our spiritual understanding. This led us to explore alternative practices such as Plant Medicine, Reiki, Meditation, and Spiritual gatherings. Through these experiences, we discovered a whole new dimension of existence that we had previously been unaware of.

These events acted as a catalyst for our desire to serve others. We began by working with friends, utilizing our limited knowledge, but what made a difference was our genuine intention to assist others. At first, we were receptive listeners, offering a supportive ear to those needing a sounding board. As we continued our assistance, we started to awaken gifts within us due to that service. The more we served, the more we received help from the universe and high-vibrational energies that provided us with the skills to aid others.

"The true awakening to our self-realization came as a result of service."

Our journey has been stormy, filled with its share of peaks, valleys, setbacks, and failures. However, in hindsight, we see all these experiences as blessings. Throughout our trials and difficulties, we learned the significance of "honoring the process," especially when things didn't unfold as we had hoped or expected. Today, rather than view our struggles as a burden, we recognize them as necessary tools for our growth and development.

Today, we stand as the men we are because of the lessons we learned along the way, and we are grateful. But most importantly, today, we are at peace.

Meeting My Guides The Pleiadians

Our discovery of spirit guides, galactic beings, and celestial masters was only made possible through introspection. It began with a desire to explore the unknown, but in our pursuit of knowledge, we found something even more profound - ourselves.

Marco Antonio

Our journey to healing from past wounds began with a commitment to integrate and find peace with our childhood experiences. We had been carrying a lot of emotional baggage that interfered with our consciousness, so we aimed to lighten our load. That's when we consciously decided to explore beyond what we could understand.

During a trip to Las Vegas, we met a woman who shared our interest in plant medicine and referred us to a shaman in Florida, where we live. Through participating in shamanic rituals, we discovered Ayahuasca, a sacred plant that allowed us to go deep into our psyche. However, the healing process took work, and as we continued with the ceremonies, it became increasingly challenging.

For the next couple of years, and after participating in these sacred Ayahuasca rituals several times during a ceremony, I asked the shaman, "It's been five ceremonies; why am I still suffering so much? Shouldn't it be easier?." He explained that it was the other way around. The deeper you go, the harder it gets. Like peeling an onion, the medicine works in layers until it reaches the core, where the most profound wounds reside. Therefore, the deeper we go, the harder it becomes to heal.

We maintained our involvement in diverse rituals, and spiritual assemblies to strengthen our path. On the eve preceding our 42nd birthday, we embarked on a journey to Castle Lake, a majestic mountain in Southern California. There, we partook in a transformative two-day Ayahuasca ceremony, and on the second night, the medicine revealed its gentle nature for the first time. In a profound state of gratitude and introspection, I meditated upon the snowy landscape, fixating on the stars that seemingly formed a mesmerizing cluster, giving rise to the illusion of containment.

At approximately 3:00 AM, and despite the chill in the air, the mountain bestowed upon me a comforting warmth. However, my tranquility became disrupted by the sensation of being watched. Swiftly, without a moment's delay, I pivoted, scanning my surroundings, but all that met my gaze were the trees and the familiar path leading to the cabin. Aware that it was time to rejoin the group, I proceeded forward, constantly glancing over my shoulder, assuring that no one was behind me. After ensuring I was alone, I redirected my gaze forward, only to witness a sight that would serve as my guiding force in the coming years.

Two ethereal beings, radiating a humanoid form, hovered gracefully in the air, resembling "twins." Their translucent figures exuded a gentle, light blue hue and average stature. Although lacking distinct facial features, they emanated an aura of profound Love, evoking a serene sense of tranquility within me. Although I was under the effects of the medicine, what I was witnessing wasn't a vision as my eyes were wide open; not a shred of fear gripped my being, and I basked in an overwhelming sense of calm and profound ease.

At that precise moment, a telepathic connection ensued, enabling me to comprehend their every thought instantaneously. I recall asking, "Why have you revealed yourselves to me?" To what they replied within my mind, "You perceive our presence because your vibrational frequency resonates with gratitude, the highest resonance upon planet Earth."

I always believed that 'love' held the highest vibrational frequency on Earth," I responded. They clarified the profound nature of Love, providing a comprehensive illustration of its all-encompassing essence and significance, vanishing soon after this transmission.

As they vanished, an overwhelming urge compelled me to implore, "No, please don't leave! I have so many questions." Filled with awe and urgency, I returned to the cabin, eager to share my extraordinary encounter with the medicine woman overseeing the ceremony. Yet, as I told the details, a look of disbelief washed over her face. She suggested, "Perhaps they were the spirits of the mountains." But without hesitation, I responded, "No, they were not spirits; they were extraterrestrial beings."

Shortly after that, a voice resonated within my mind - it was an intuitive understanding to return outside. Sensing the significance of this call, I told the shaman woman, "they are asking me to come back out." So I asked her and my brother to join me this time. The three of us approached the door and swung it open, only to be greeted by the chilly night air and a porch leading to a flag billowing inconsistently in the wind. As we scanned the surroundings, they were nowhere to be seen. We stood there in contemplation, and then my brother suggested, "Perhaps their intention is to only engage with you." before he retreated inside. Acknowledging his words, the medicine woman nodded in agreement and followed him back into the cabin.

I found myself alone once again, only this time, accompanied by a sense of unease. At that moment, I courageously expressed, "I am here, scared but willing to take the first step." - In response, a reassuring voice echoed within me, offering guidance, "That is all you are required to do, taking the first step; and we will help you take the second and every other step after." the telepathic voice in my head suggested."

Filled with determination to embark on this extraordinary journey, I took my first steps, sensing an unprecedented force guiding my every movement. A peculiar connection seemed to manifest through the flag, swaying unpredictably in the wind as if the beings were communicating through its motion. Curious, I asked, " What do you want from me?" Astonishingly, as if conjured by magic, the flag unfolded before me, revealing the resounding message, "*COEXIST.*" Surprised, I ventured further, seeking clarification, "Do you wish to coexist with me?" Their message echoed with profound significance in response: "No, we seek to coexist within you." From that moment onward, my life underwent a transformative shift beyond the realm of my imagination. Countless doors opened, revealing experiences that I had never fathomed I would encounter.

As the ceremony neared its conclusion on the following day, a woman approached me. With a curious expression, she inquired, "You encountered the beings, didn't you?" Taken aback by her question, I responded, "Yes, I did. But who are they?" Her reply was vague, "They are the Pleiadians." Although she did not disclose extensive details, she revealed that they, too, served as her guides.

Meeting My Guides Metatron

I Am Evolution in Divine Action.
Within us lies a wondrous "self" we frequently ignore, yet it holds profound magnificence. Within the heart lies absolute liberation, for it alone unleashes our infinite power. With a focused intention, empowered action unfolds, leading us to the pinnacle of our reality's potential.

Miguel Angel

Meeting my highest guide remains an unforgettable event. In California, I joined an Ayahuasca ceremony on Arrowhead Mountain. As I meditated after drinking the medicine, a peaceful silence enveloped me. I heard only my heartbeat, awakening something magical within. Then, guided by a higher power, I stepped onto the freezing cabin's balcony, greeted by a physical, giant ball of fire in the sky. It was as if I could almost touch it based on its proximity to me.

A resounding male voice from the fireball proclaimed: "I Am the Alpha and the Omega. I Am the Beginning and the End. I Am Lord Metatron." In that instant, my body straightened, my right arm raised with an open palm, while my left arm rested behind my back as if honoring the supreme consciousness of the universe. Curiously, I inquired, "Who are you?" The voice replied, "I Am the One you serve." Overwhelmed with awe and anger, I declared, "I serve no one." Yet, a subtle inner urging compelled me to remain and to lend an ear to the voice for a bit longer. A cascade of poetic words ensued from the commanding yet calming presence, and I surrendered entirely to the enchanting realm of that mystical encounter.

The fiery energy above ignited an outstanding choreography within me. With graceful subtlety reminiscent of Tai Chi, I moved in harmony. Empowered and serene, I merged seamlessly with this consciousness. The significance of Metatron unfolded, and I grasped that I am, I have always been, and forever will be, "it," the highest and the lowest, the positive and the negative, the good and the bad, and every duality or possibility there is. At that moment, my existence transcended, embracing absolute certainty—I am the entirety of All That Is.

Having settled into a state of tranquility, I ventured out of the cabin and sought a vantage point on the mountain to behold its grandeur. Yet, the scenery appeared surreal, like a shimmering hologram. Fear unsettled me, so I addressed Metatron, "Why me?" A deep-rooted feeling of unworthiness permeated my being in the face of this extraordinary event. However, once more, a surge of energy flowed within, bestowing me with a profound realization—I needed to embrace trust.

While gazing up at the celestial fireball, Metatron's consciousness persisted, offering guidance. "I will impart three teachings," he proclaimed.

"First, I will show you how to cleanse the house." Instantly, I comprehended his reference to transmuting the energy of the ceremony participants within the cabin. "Secondly," he continued, "I will teach you to elevate the mountain's frequency." Doubt crept in as I struggled to grasp the significance of this statement. Unfazed, the voice persisted, "Lastly, I will instruct you on raising the planet's frequency." Overwhelmed, I snapped out of my meditative state, overcome with disbelief. "I am nobody," I answered angrily. "Who do you think I am? Look at me! I lack qualifications and any understanding of what that entails. I am short, hailing from Mexico! I don't even comprehend why I said that, but I needed him to acknowledge my insignificance in relation to the task he had proposed."

No response reached my ears, leaving a profound silence that allowed me to regain composure. In that stillness, a deep realization unfolded—I comprehended that elevating the planet's frequency entailed raising my frequency, which would inevitably ripple outward and affect the world's energy. A sense of unity with the universe permeated my being as it became apparent that I embodied the essence of the cosmos. If I could transform within myself, I possessed the power to influence the frequency of all that surrounded me, bestowing me a profound sense of tranquility.

Encountering Metatron proved to be a remarkable and life-altering experience. A profound shift in consciousness ensued, endowing me with an unprecedented sense of responsibility. I embraced self-sufficiency and self-realization, comprehending the potency of becoming the wellspring from which all desired manifestations could arise. I no longer sought external saviors; instead, I harnessed the power within myself. At last, I attained absolute mastery over my life, guided by unwavering clarity that I possessed the ability to change and manifest anything I desired from the depths of my being.

After the Ayahuasca ceremony, returning to Miami on the plane, I felt more confused and had more questions than ever before. I was frustrated because I didn't want to rely on plant medicine to access the deep wisdom I experienced during the ceremonies. I looked out the window for the fireball in the sky but saw nothing. I dropped my head in disappointment for a while with no thoughts. Then, after a few seconds, a surge of energy revitalized my entire body, and I sat upright in a lotus position, feeling Metatron's powerful presence. Luckily, I had an empty seat beside me, granting my body the freedom to move and resonate with the universal rhythm. The experience persisted for hours, and an inner certainty emerged that my life would transform permanently.

In the subsequent days, at 3:00 AM, Metatron entered my energy field, acquainting me with Yoga and revealing teachings on sacred geometry through physical expression. Following this, a profound shift occurred within my consciousness, granting me the understanding that I could deliberately connect with the "Divine source" whenever I desired.

Lord Metatron became the catalyst for a profound transformation in my life. Whenever I connect with his essence, he greets me with a loving invitation to engage in interaction. Then, with compassionate wisdom, he delivers messages that are precisely what I need every time, offering his perspective filled with love. Yet, he consistently concludes each statement by affirming, "This is simply an invitation, and the choice to accept or decline is entirely yours."

In the present day, my life resonates with self-sufficiency as I discover that all the answers lie within. I feel boundless love, profound compassion, unwavering support, and every essential element dwelling within me. I embody the abundance of Divine empowerment, liberating myself from the role of a mere victim in my narrative.

We are the Arcturians

When your Intention is to "Expand"
Expantion Happens.

Upon encountering The Pleiadians and Metatron during plant medicine in the mountains, we returned to Miami with awe and curiosity. Seeking guidance, we aligned with individuals who willingly shared their wisdom without asking. A woman approached us during one of the meditation circles we participated in. Her face was astonished, and she said, "You both radiate a remarkably potent Arcturian energy."

"The Arcturians?" We inquired, - "Yes, the Arcturians serve as my guides," briefly explaining their essence. However, our connection lies with the Pleiadians; we replied" with a sense of pride. Little did we know, this chance encounter introduced us to the consciousness of beings that would become our mentors and the source of great teachings over the forthcoming years.

Our initial encounter with the Arcturian consciousness occurred almost simultaneously for my twin and me. However, they presented themselves as individual entities rather than a collective consciousness during that period. As our evolutionary journey progressed, we came to comprehend that they are indeed celestial beings possessing distinctive qualities, constituting a profoundly elevated vibrational consciousness.

Miguel's Connection

My connection happened in the middle of the night, during my sleep. I was suddenly awakened by the deep resonance of a powerful, masculine voice that declared, "We are the Arcturians." Initially, I questioned whether I was immersed in a dream, as I never felt or heard that before. Yet, the voice resonated once more, emanating profound affection, reiterating, "We are the Arcturians." This time, beyond a mere introduction, it felt like an invitation to establish a connection with them. In response, my physical form instinctively rose, and my hands joined upon my forehead, assuming a prayerful gesture.

For the next several seconds, my body remained immobile, not out of paralysis, but rather because that energy resonated harmoniously within my heart. In that very instant, I sensed a loving invitation to embark upon this profound bond as I connected with these light beings for the first time.

Marco's Connection

My encounter unfolded similarly to my twin brother's, only the day after his introduction, although slightly different. Around 3:00 AM, while I was sleeping, I was awakened by a commanding voice that resonated within my soul; my body rose, and my hands instinctively assumed a prayerful position on my forehead. The determined voice echoed threefold: "We are the Arcturians, we are the Arcturians, we are the Arcturians." They sought to establish their identity within my consciousness, ensuring I comprehended who they were.

Immediately after that, my voice echoed the precise phrase three times: "I am an Arcturian, I am an Arcturian, I am an Arcturian." Let it be clear that I do not seek to imply my own Arcturian origin. Yet, at that moment, I experienced such profound alignment with this energy that I merged with it, embodying the essence itself.

Today, we have come to comprehend that our connection extends beyond individual entities but interweaving with a collective consciousness. Following those memorable nights, similar events unfolded in our lives over the following months, predominantly occurring during the nighttime hours. An innate sense of ease pervaded these encounters, evoking familiarity and deep comfort. Never did it produce any act of threat or unease.

Whenever we would feel their energy, it would be at approximately 3:30 AM. Our hands gracefully glide in circular patterns across our foreheads and heart chakras during those moments. Our bodies would instinctively adopt irregular movements whose significance we didn't understand. Yet, the sensation felt that a profound energy work was being conducted.
During those times, the concepts of chakra alignments and energy were foreign to our understanding. Nevertheless, our hands became the vessel through which we retained and recalled this hidden wisdom that resonated deeply within our entire being.

However, their impact on us went beyond mere energetic influence and extended to our physical selves. On numerous occasions, we found ourselves assuming unfamiliar bodily postures, unlocking the potential of our physical beings and immersing ourselves in an entirely new realm of existence. Curiosity arose within us, prompting the question, "What are you doing?" Yet, this inquiry was not born out of doubt but rather from a place of unwavering trust and surrender. The voice that echoed in our minds consistently responded, "We are prolonging your life because we require your presence on this planet for a little longer than you expect."

This profound realization deeply touched both of us, as we realized that maybe what we do matters and today, we grasp the true essence of their message. And not because we believe we are "Arcturians." On the contrary, we embrace our humanity; however, for the first time, we felt a profound sense of purpose and an overwhelming desire to contribute in a greater capacity.

After that point, our knowledge expanded to manipulating energy through intention within ourselves and others. We received guidance and visual demonstrations, helping us grasp the techniques for working with individuals, resulting in extraordinary outcomes. Surprisingly, we eventually established a systematic approach. Nevertheless, our methods remain unique as we tailor our facilitated sessions to suit each person. In essence, we have developed an intuitive system.

We acknowledge the desire for individuals to connect with higher energies, and our constant reminder is that such connections are established through acts of service. Before our encounter with this elevated state of awareness, we were already on a path of service, and it was through their benevolence that these higher vibrational frequencies extended their assistance to us. However, it is essential to note that our perspective and connection with these entities are subjective and unique to our experience and not the only way to do it.

I AM YOU
Higher-Self

I am your innermost guide, your mastery.
I am your companion and your strength.
I am your highs, but I am also there during your lows.
I am the presence you feel but cannot see, expressed at every moment.

I am your essence, your being, your soul, and beyond.
I am as apparent as nature itself, although not of a physical appearance.
I shine in you and through you. Always present, but I have also been there in your past and will be there in your future. Here, now and then.

I am your most loving friend but also your most prominent teacher.
I come from one source - the highest source. The source we are all part of and one.
I am always aware of your emotions, thoughts, and feelings.
I am your state of consciousness.

We are not separate; we are one merged by the cosmic glue that brings us all together. You are me, and I am you. In essence, we are one.

I am more extensive than the mind's capacity to understand, as I am not to be understood but felt and fully integrated.
I am here to support the reality you have chosen to experience in this lifetime. So rest assured and rest free; live passionately and lovingly.

You are on the right path.
Trust the universe within and the divine plan you are a part of now.
Because the entire universe - trusts you.

Your Higher-Self

The Concept of
ONENESS

"When you recognize yourself as ONE with the highest source, you must become the conscious channel of that source."

As identical twins from a very young age, we were introduced to the profound notion of Oneness and gained a deep understanding of what it truly meant to be reflections of one another. We were perfect mirrors, similar to the "Yin and Yang." This awareness began in our mother's womb, experiencing what it's like to be one seed that fractalized into two separate and unique beings.

The concept of mirroring extends to all individuals we encounter in our journey. What we perceive in others is merely an aspect of ourselves that reminds us of our ongoing evolutionary path. When we recognize love and compassion in others, we first acknowledge these qualities within ourselves. Contrarily, when we realize their opposites, we see them reflected in us.

Moreover, we comprehended that all ascended masters, angels, galactic entities, and higher vibrational beings are also aspects of us. We all emanate from a singular source, expressing itself through infinite fractals, each experiencing existence. As we learned how to channel and establish connections with higher-frequency beings, it became evident that these connections were mirrors of our essence. It doesn't imply that these high-vibrational beings lack their unique expressions; rather, it signifies that we no longer perceive ourselves as separate from them.

Grasping the concept of Oneness requires introspection and the realization that you are one with the divine source, the very presence you've been seeking all along. You possess all the tools needed for this journey, "especially the heart." Embracing this divinity within you triggers a shift in consciousness, forging a connection to the most crucial master, "Yourself."

Oneness beyond a concept is a state of awareness, "a frequency." When you attune yourself to this frequency, you realize you are the master of your destiny, the Buddha of the future, the universe itself. Oneness ceases to be a mere notion; it becomes an intrinsic part of your being, imprinted into your cellular structure, and the illusion of separation dissolves.

You are now ready to activate your inner connectivity technology. This activation signifies a conscious acceptance that we are one, all fragments of the same source that birthed everything, existing within us, not outside.

You are not Alone!

There is an old consciousness concept that says:
"We come alone, and we leave alone."
You feel separate from the divine source when you're not entirely giving yourself to your life's purpose. Only at that moment does the feeling of emptiness create the illusion of loneliness.

When you choose to incarnate on this planet, you embark on a mission orchestrated by a divine source that supports you at all times, and above all, you are inherently connected to this source. This support network, comprised of unseen energies, remains alongside you throughout your earthly journey, and we refer to these energies as spirit guides.

Your presence on Earth serves a profound purpose that only you can fulfill. These spiritual guides diligently ensure your guidance and alignment with the right path while you are here.

Your arrival on Earth is neither random nor accidental; you synchronize with a divine purpose and mission that empowers you to shape your reality consistently. Throughout your time on this planet, you retain the ability to choose your path, and hopefully, one day, you realize that you are the very essence of this purpose. Whether conscious of it or not, you are supported throughout your life.

As you conclude your earthly journey and transcend, you depart surrounded by your family and loved ones. At the moment of your transcendence, your universal family is already present, eagerly awaiting to guide you back home or wherever your journey leads.

You don't come alone; you are never alone, and don't leave this world alone. Yet, the occasional loneliness we experience is as ancient as the act of creation itself. When the universal creative source emerged from an eternal meditative state, it found itself "alone" (within the void), recognizing that it was "All That Is," yet still solitary as the One Infinite Consciousness.

The original thought of this source creator was "to experience itself." And so, it fragmented infinitely to contemplate itself and escape the feeling of "solitude." So, this original feeling of loneliness resides in our souls and spirit.

"I AM YOU" is a remembrance that you are eternally linked to every energy, Master, or spirit guide within this divine support system, as you are inherently one with them. You represent a unique aspect of God's creative source, to which we all belong and shall ultimately return.

The Polarity System

Your Higher Self - Emotional Balance; and how they relate to the Human Experience.

What is the one quality we know about energy? Energy can neither be created nor destroyed; it exists; it always has and will always be. When energy moves, it doesn't do it in a linear direction; it spins and expands in a circular motion "like waves."

So when energy spins, let's say "up" and to the right, it must reflect "down" and to the left, creating an opposite "mirrored version of itself." This energy reflection always exists alternately to create balance; otherwise, the system would collapse. This process is the beginning of alternate realities, except they are both aware of each other's existence at energy levels. They are in continuous communication and innately connected; they are perfect opposites.

As an individual, you are part of the whole. So, whenever there's an alteration to the whole, the opposite must reflect and mirror the change.

Also, at a personal level, alternative realities are created. So when we make choices, the opposite/counter-event is created simultaneously. So, by frequency and focus, we decide which events we want to partake in, and a different aspect will experience the other. So the more "Aware" we are and the more we know how energy and reality work, the more we can connect to higher aspects of reality. The more we can vibrate at higher frequencies. However, if our "awareness" level is low, we will reflect lower vibrational experiences and connect to the contrasting version of reality we want to manifest. See image below

High Vibrational Frequencies

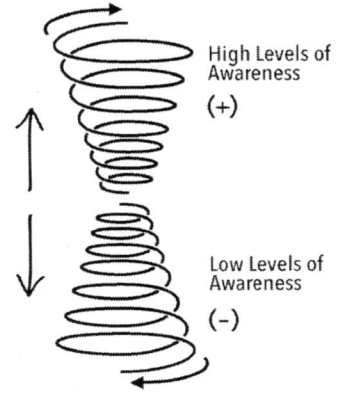

High Levels of Awareness
(+)

Low Levels of Awareness
(−)

Low Vibrational Frequencies

The concept of opposites compares to conversing with someone in a completely different time or space. You can be on opposite sides of the planet at other times and still be connected and have a conversation on the phone. At that one moment, time and space are only an illusion. Time zones are an example of how alternate realities of time and space are happening simultaneously, and we are unaware of them.

The Emotional Body

Vibrating at a low frequency does not make anyone a "bad" person; it only means that they are not "focusing their attention" at that moment on higher levels of existence. And even sometimes, "aware" individuals can experience lower vibration levels if they focus on those frequencies. Because of the agenda of the 3rd dimension, we can visit both aspects and ride that "rollercoaster" of the human experience, the "emotional ride."

There are about 108 emotions in human existence. Because we cannot see this system or have a way to measure our vibratory frequency, we can measure our vibration levels by the type of events we are experiencing. We are walking reflectors, manifesting a reality based on these vibratory levels. Are you experiencing high or low vibrational events in your life? Events in your life are a clear indicator and an accurate way to determine whether you are vibrating high or low.

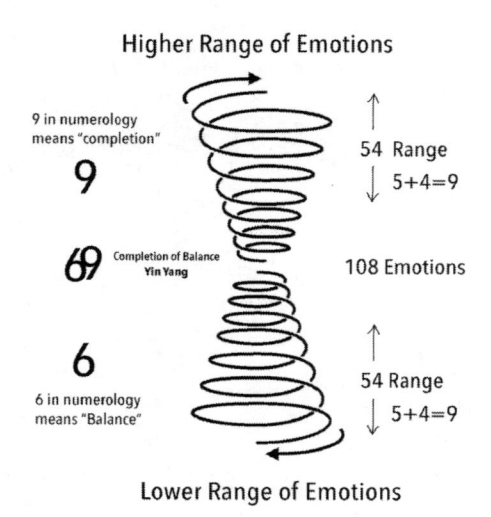

Higher Range of Emotions

9 in numerology means "completion"

9

54 Range
5+4=9

Completion of Balance
Yin Yang

108 Emotions

6

6 in numerology means "Balance"

54 Range
5+4=9

Lower Range of Emotions

Higher Self - Your higher and lower self are one, are connected, and support each other. The difference is that the Higher Self is "Aware" of that connection and support. In contrast, the lower self supports the Higher Self "unconsciously" as they are part of a universal and perfect system (Lower systems support higher systems; the same as lower dimensions support higher dimensions).

Even though your lower self is not aware of alternative timelines, your Higher Self is at all times. Therefore, your Higher aspect does not exist in a different realm or the future; another version of you exists simultaneously here and now.

Calling upon or connecting to your Higher Self is a natural state of being, not a process. However, it is best to consciously detach from lower emotional drama and frequencies to connect to it. To raise your vibrational frequency, you must connect to - positive thoughts, emotions and feelings.

When you bring all emotions to balance and connect to higher vibrational emotions, you feel the connection with your Higher Self at a conscious level. The more "Aware" you become and commit to your heightened vibrational emotions, the less you experience lower aspects of existence.

It does not mean that lower aspects will no longer exist; it only means that you are not focused or attached to them. Ultimately, the events in your life that make you uncomfortable or overwhelmed are what you came here to experience. These events are where learning exists and what will give you the mastery that will teach you compassion and love for yourself during the integration process.

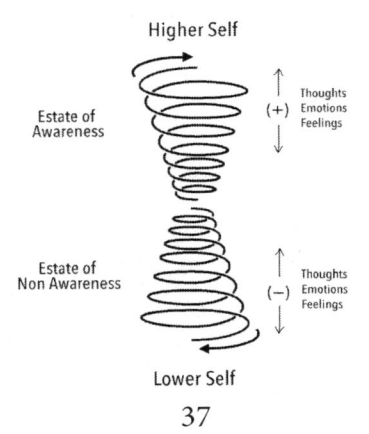

Higher Self

Estate of Awareness   (+) Thoughts Emotions Feelings

Estate of Non Awareness   (−) Thoughts Emotions Feelings

Lower Self

You,
your Higher-Self
& Higher Aspects

When you know yourself to be your higher self, there is no longer a need to "connect" because you already are at every moment.

Living in your higher self involves embracing and allowing the experience of elevated aspects of yourself that we sometimes suppress. It's crucial to recognize that your higher self isn't a distinct entity separate from you. To desire to melde with your higher self implies a disconnection that doesn't inherently exist; it assumes there's a process to establish this connection.

In reality, you perpetually reside within your higher self. Believing otherwise generates a false sense of separation and triggers feelings of inadequacy. This false perception of dual aspects—higher and lower selves - misconceives the unity within your being.

Your essence is not inherently dualistic; this is merely an illusion. At a universal level, your being encompasses everything and comprehends itself as all-encompassing. When you begin to act, think, and feel from this profound understanding, there's no need to strive for a connection with your "higher self" or "higher aspects" because you are them.

Your higher self doesn't manifest exclusively during meditation or moments of silence. The "I AM" is your higher, lower, and infinite self; you are a singular expression manifesting continuously, although recognition of this unity typically occurs at heightened levels of consciousness.

Elevating your frequency facilitates the experience of this "connection" and a sense of unity. This elevated state of awareness expands you across various levels of consciousness.

An infinite array of expressions emanates from the singular source you can connect with, such as Galactic beings, Angelic energies, Spiritual guides, and other facets of the Divine. These entities and energies are "higher expressions of consciousness," a consciousness that resides in you. Despite their distinctive qualities, they are integral aspects of your being. We are all united by an invisible force that binds us all together.

Oneness Mantra
I honor the aspect of me that exists in you
I honor the aspect of you that exists in me
And allow the majesty of our spirits to merge as One.

Let the Message come from Silence

There is a void that contains every answer you've been searching for.

You are invited to engage with the profound wisdom residing within you by embracing the serenity of silence. Within this tranquil space, a unique sound known only to you communicates a wealth of guidance, insight, and clarity. When you listen, the voice of silence can deliver information without words and with the elegance of the Cosmos.

Listen with all your senses and emotions; there is no need to rush to get your desired information. All the guidance and information you wish to channel is engraved in your DNA, cellular structure, and part of your innate. There's no need for audible guidance; instead, permit the messages to flow through you unexpectedly and surprisingly. They will always be presented to you in a manner that aligns with your own comprehension and level of understanding.

Messages may arrive in unanticipated forms; information has infinite avenues of revelation. Silence, mainly when you exist in a state of openness, is a magnificent medium of expression. The void embodies guidance and can manifest itself in manners beyond your imagination.

There is so much information in silence, breathing consciously, being at peace, and simply being present. When you stop listening to the chatter in your head, the voice of silence can be heard.

Higher vibrational energies seldom employ words; instead, they convey understanding that seamlessly integrates with your entire being. In essence, the voice of silence cannot be explained; it is to be felt and absorbed at a conscious level, transcending the limitations of a thousand words or any language.

Listening to the voice of silence is jumping into greatness without a parachute, merging with your inner wisdom, the same knowledge of the universe. Find confidence in surrendering to this path, knowing that once you silence the mind, there is no turning back.

As you assume responsibility for your mastery and embrace silence, you become a conduit and messenger of infinite love, awareness, and endless possibilities.

The Promise

To assist other StarSeeds doing spiritual work to remember who they are and why they are here. And most importantly, it is to help them in their journeys to go to their next level of evolution at a mental, emotional, physical, and spiritual level.
And this is the promise.

Our first contact with celestial beings was with a consciousness called The Arcturians. The connection happened in the middle of the night while we were asleep. At approximately 3:00 AM, a voice woke us, saying, "We are the Arcturians." Astonishingly, this voice emanated from our mouths and repeated this declaration three times, ensuring we comprehended their identity. This event happened individually to both of us in our separate rooms but simultaneously during the night.

Initially, we found ourselves overwhelmed, yet an exhilaration rushed through us as we witnessed our lives transform before our very eyes. During our energy sessions, we learned to work with the Chakra system, access the Akashic records, Merkaba traveling, activate the Third Eye, and other tools. Even though these newfound gifts arose from our dedication to assisting others, we couldn't help but question: Why us.?

We had never received formal training or initiation into any energy healing modality. So when we asked these beings, we received a response: "It is because you are empty vessels; you have no reference of preconceived notions from old conditioning or entangled belief systems. Your lack of prior knowledge is why you are ideal conduits for embracing this new consciousness of revelation and transformation." We were only required to be present and in a state of openness, allowing universal energy to flow through us and extend assistance.

We remember our first group session; we were nervous, and we didn't know how we would perform the work they said we could do. Once more, the inner voice planted a seed of wisdom in our minds, declaring: There are two things you need to know to do this work, and if you live by these two things, you'll never question yourself again. *"It is all within you & There is no wrong way to do it."*

We learned to allow the energy work to flow through us during our sessions rather than believing it was "from us." From that day onward, these words became integral to our being, resonating within us every time. When we trust and surrender ourselves to our service, we constantly feel the support and aid of a legion of light beings and masters who made us a solemn promise: *"The work you're required to do it's already done; you just have to be present and go through the process."*

What is Channeling?

Channeling means elevating your frequency so high
that you become aware of higher aspects of existence.
And from this awareness,
express yourself as one with them.

Channeling is adapt your own body to the vibration of the information you want to receive. It is consciously connecting to a higher aspect of the creative source. By surrendering control of the mind, you open a pathway to access universal knowledge that flows through your heart center. You can express this wisdom from this source in any chosen form, whether the spoken word, singing, painting, or playing an instrument. You are, in essence, a conduit for this creative force, even when you are not consciously aware of it.

Everything you say, think and feel connects to a vibrational frequency (high or low). Therefore, when you experience emotions of gratitude, joy, and abundance, you are, at that moment, a vessel for these elevated frequencies. As a result, these inner resonances manifest in your external reality. Conversely, the same principle applies to lower vibrational emotions and feelings.

Channeling beings of higher vibrational energy is an act of love, accomplished through focused intention and a conscious connection with your heart's core. This process enables higher aspects of existence to manifest through you. Furthermore, channeling is a consequence of your dedication to serving others, maintaining a pure diet, and cultivating a clear mind.

It is relevant to mention that the distinction between channeling emotions and "conscious channeling" relates to your intention, state of being, awareness, and how you feel about yourself at every moment.

The entirety of wisdom resides within you, connecting with "All That Is" in the vast Universe. When you engage in conscious channeling, you are essentially remembering. You are in harmony with the boundless facets of the "All"; thus, the information and connection you receive emanate from a higher aspect of your being.

Channeling allows you to serve as a vessel for communication; it involves embodying both the message and the messenger simultaneously. Channeling allows information to flow without judgment, enabling your heart's rhythm to translate these frequencies into guidance. Channeling is a skill that improves with practice. The more you engage in it, the more effortless it becomes. Channeling - Trusting - Becoming - Being.

What is Meditation?

Meditation is surrendering to the present moment like the sunset surrenders to the horizon, offering no resistance and allowing the most profound void to be the canvas of your wildest dreams.

In our understanding and personal experience, meditation is a practice of self-love. It's an adventurous ride into the subconscious mind and a journey where we can experience the magic that we are. It's the art of becoming the universe's wisdom while you allow yourself to dive into the most beautiful realms of existence.

In meditation, boundless possibilities materialize; through this process, we realize our fullest potential. In meditation, we transcend boundaries and become masters of our existence. We discover answers to life's mysteries, and as long as we can cultivate relaxation and well-being, we find clarity in the domain of the Divine.

But how can we know if we have entered the meditative state? Assuming a lotus position with closed eyes does not guarantee meditation. However, aligning our physical selves into the tetrahedron shape "legs crossed" allows us to resonate and connect with other dimensions of our being. It sets the process in motion, and the journey begins.
You know you have entered the meditative state when your breath cycles slow down, becoming brief and serene. It's a profound tranquility, bordering on a deep trance and blissful serenity.

Meditation means surrendering to the present moment and allowing your mind to rest while you become empty of thoughts and feelings. In meditation, your goal is to become emotionless and neutral, like the universe. At that moment, you experience the entirety of the universe within.

Conversely, you can sense that you are not in meditation or giving your mind rest when the images you encounter are mere recreations of the egoic mind rather than clear visions accessed through the third eye. The distinction lies in the mind's ability to manipulate self-created images, whereas images accessed through the third eye appear as naturally as opening one's eyes.

You will enter the Theta state of consciousness once you attain a profound state of relaxation. It is within this state that heightened awareness and vivid visualization unfold. When you reach the Theta state, you gain a newfound clarity and tap into your inner wisdom. Naturally, the journey progresses through the Beta and Alpha states of awareness before arriving at Theta, but this is where dedicated practice plays a crucial role.

A light diet

All food contains an energetic, emotional weight for the soul and an energetic weight for the body. This energy becomes part of your pattern, structure, and being and part of your cellular stability and fundamental elements. "You are what you eat."

During meditation, a pivotal consideration is what you feed your body. Hence, before striving to channel information with clarity, it is essential to be as "light" as possible. Being light means being on an empty stomach or eating foods that are not excessively heavy and dense.

A diet based on fruits, vegetables, and grains can supply your body with essential nutrients, minerals, and elements your cells require for optimal functioning. So, in your pursuit of stability within your cells to sustain their peak performance and expansion, it is imperative to source these elements from organisms in your external environment that are "alive."

When you consume dense foods such as meat, poultry, or fish (dead animal products), you become more dense as you eat heavier. You absorb their physical weight, the potential toxins, and emotional and energetic residue.

We are not advocating a shift in your dietary habits expecting you to become a vegetarian or vegan overnight. Before doing this, it is advisable to seek the guidance of a nutritionist who can tailor recommendations to your body's specific needs. Each body is unique and may require different dietary approaches. We propose a gradual change in your eating habits that helps you become lighter to achieve better results.

When ready to embark on a journey of channeling and connection, ensure you are well-hydrated. Some of our most profound insights have occurred while sticking to a liquid diet. Our bodies are exceptionally light during such moments, facilitating connections with unparalleled ease and clarity. We firmly believe that achieving a state of "enlightenment" is less about meditation per se and more about the "lightness" of your physical being.

Once again, this is only our process and experience when connecting with higher frequencies. This approach has assisted us in assimilating information and tapping into inner wisdom during deep meditation.

Embracing a heightened level of consciousness reveals that we are, in many ways, a reflection of what we consume. Choosing vibrant foods becomes imperative if you aspire to connect deeper. In this context, detoxifying your diet is essential to purifying your mind and spirit, seeking inner peace, and unlocking dormant abilities.

Creating a Sacred Space

Create a sacred space in your heart first.
A harmonious temple is a state of being.
And when you're able to access that place of serenity within,
you become your sanctuary.

Creating a sacred space is essential for meditation and the connection journey. Find a quiet place at home where you can feel comfortable and at peace; make sure it's private so you won't be interrupted or distracted. A harmonious setting facilitates a profound connection. You can incorporate gentle music, candles, incense, flowers, crystals, or cherished images.

Items that arouse happiness and inner tranquility are ideal for adorning your altar or meditation sanctuary. They symbolize your resonance with specific energies and ideals but are not prerequisites for generating a connection.

Utilize cushions for more comfortable seating and maintain relaxation, adjusting your posture as needed. Never compromise your comfort during meditation, like back pain or numbness in your legs. The duration of your meditation is your preference and will vary each time.

Silence is imperative to cultivate an optimal meditation atmosphere. However, if you intend to meditate, you can still find inner peace and calm the noise in your mind, even sitting in a park surrounded by noise. This approach is mainly contingent on meditation being a well-practiced daily ritual and your proficiency as an advanced practitioner.

For instance, we wrote this book's content through meditating primarily within the confines of our home. However, we've also received insights while hiking or climbing in the mountains by meditating at the beach or away in a cabin for days, consciously connecting to retrieve information.

Once, during meditation, Goddess Isis expressed, "Rituals are beautiful but not necessary - it's all about the intention." In other words, you can create an exceptional space, yet profound connections can happen without an altar or tools at any corner of your home.

Even in the middle of the night, we've been woken up and received insights and information from celestial beings or other energies. So, more than a favored place, the connection starts with you; you're the holy temple.

The place or space you select for meditation is a deeply personal choice. There is no definitive right or wrong spot to connect; as long as you're grounded and at peace, you become your sacred space.

Tools & Objects

Acknowledging who you are
will give you access to the wisdom you are.
You are the Tool,
You are the Guidance,
You are the Connection.

In the initial stages of our channeling and connection journey, we were encouraged to refrain from relying on external tools or objects. That included plant medicine, crystals, amulets, mandalas, music, guided meditations, or any "shortcuts" to facilitate the connection. The emphasis was on recognizing ourselves as the primary instrument for channeling and connecting.

While it's perfectly acceptable to incorporate items like sage, palo santo, scented oils, or music to set the mood, do it out of genuine love for the experience rather than as a means to propel a connection. The journey is about achieving a sense of well-being. Therefore, not giving absolute authority to tools or objects is essential because, at that moment, you're giving your power away.

Once you attain a profound connection through meditation and acknowledge yourself as the primary tool, you can integrate other instruments like plant medicine, crystals, mantras, or anything supporting your channeling process.

Plant medicine played a crucial role in our journey, but after several years of connecting without external aids, they entered our lives. This invitation to engage with sacred plants was not to enhance the connection but to experience it from a different perspective. Through this process, we realized that it's not the medicine men or women who work with sacred plants but those who have recognized themselves as the medicine itself.

When we began our conscious service, we would visit the beach (our sacred space at the time). Our primary tool was our ability to empathetically listen to people's struggles, which made a significant difference to them. Over time, our hands developed the capacity to sense which chakras needed attention. Eventually, we started receiving visualizations and insights into universal concepts previously unknown to us.

The more we dedicated ourselves to assisting others, the more we unlocked abilities within ourselves. It became evident that the higher energies we were connecting with were awakening the inherent gifts necessary for our work in helping others. Ultimately, we became acutely aware that we were the sole instrument required to establish a connection and channel higher vibrational frequencies.

The Power of Intention

What you focus on will bring upon the celestial teachers of that mastery to support your commitment and intention.

Your intention serves as the blueprint for your desires, sparking the engine of the manifestation process. Your determination to attain and fulfill your purpose sets in motion the essential events that lead you toward the desired journey.

An intention starts with asking yourself specific questions to receive exact answers. Then, focus your attention and energy on what you want to expand in your life. Your purpose for connecting and channeling involves knowing what you seek and taking action to experience your desired outcome.

Previously, we discussed the essential steps to initiate this process, such as establishing a sacred space, adopting a light diet, and recognizing your role as an instrument. These actions align with your objectives: connecting with your higher self and other elevated frequencies.

During a visit to Mt. Shasta, we advised participants that if they sought contact or communion with higher frequencies, they should make that their primary intention. Out of over 30 people, only a few had clear objectives, and the rest ignored the invitation. Those who embraced a clear purpose and took the necessary steps to materialize their intentions were the sole beneficiaries of the expected contacts and connections.

Setting an intention mirrors the commitment required for establishing goals; it entails the same unwavering dedication to propel your desires forward. You do not merely set goals and hope for them to materialize miraculously. Like shooting an arrow, you must concentrate and exert sufficient effort to provide the energy needed to propel it in your desired direction and strike your target.

When you establish intentions of the highest and purest caliber, you elevate your frequency, instantly attracting the support required from energies resonating at that same frequency.

Consequently, when your intentions align with high vibrational states, you receive assistance from energies resonating at a similar frequency throughout your journey. The same happens when what you wish for is of the opposite frequency. So, your vibrational and emotional states are the key when setting goals to manifest your objectives.

Trust Yourself

Allow the wisdom that comes through you to be from a place of trust. You are a pure channel; the information you receive can only happen from a space of certainty.

Initially, our spirit guides constantly reminded us to "trust" during our connection process. So every time we doubted, they would always come back and make the same invitation to "Trust the process." And so we did.

Although this invitation sounded like a beautiful reminder, we needed to learn what it meant in practical ways. So after a while, we inquired: We never questioned the guidance, but now we need a little more than that. What does "Trust the process" mean? In response, the mastery voice gently offered insight: "We asked you to trust the process because, at that time, you weren't prepared to trust yourself. Although we were urging you to place your faith in a Divine Source, it was a way to encourage you to invest that trust in the guidance you believed was leading you. Today, you are ready to integrate that "You are the Process," we invite you to place your complete trust in yourself. We have consistently urged you to trust your inner wisdom and nothing external.

Trusting yourself and the wisdom you hold within will help you become a free individual and an independent being. Knowing that you are the source of your support, clarity, guidance, and anything you're still looking for outside of you is essential.

When you fall in love with yourself and embrace your true essence, you harmonize with the universe's energies. You establish a connection and communication channel with your higher self, spiritual guides, and elevated vibrational frequencies. Trusting yourself dissolves the illusion of separation from these loving energies. You become assured that everything exists within you and is in unity with the entirety.

Sometimes, the path to accessing profound insights may appear uncertain, but this, too, is a facet of "trusting." It doesn't always have to feel effortless; sometimes, it can be challenging. True mastery lies in trusting, even when it defies logic or ventures beyond your comfort zone.

Trusting is being open to everything and knowing it all has a purpose. Your higher self invites you to trust and elevate your frequency so you can further advance in your process of evolution. All communication and information you access aligns with your vibrational level and will always be what you need to experience.

Permission & Self Validation

Today, I have decided to be loyal to my convictions. Today, I have decided to be true to myself. I am, I am, I am.

Embrace every facet of your existence that has guided you to this point. Your life is a masterpiece; it always has been and always will be. You are entitled to tap into universal wisdom; it resides within you. However, there are moments when we may require additional time to feel prepared and deserving of divine guidance or doubt our capacity to channel high vibrational energies.

Acknowledging your worthiness and permitting yourself to receive it "All" is crucial. Self-validation is an act of self-love, and no outside source can do that for you. When you ask for "guidance," you're asking for permission to attain something you believe you lack without realizing that guidance emerges from your inner being.

It is essential to nurture self-esteem, declare clearly, "I lovingly grant myself permission to..." and affirm your intention; this isn't a request but your information and divine birthright. Release all expectations and give yourself everything with love, expecting nothing yet open to everything. The connection and insight you receive do not originate externally; they are creations of your innermost self.

By validating yourself and aligning with your "Being" and "I AM Presence," the path unfolds before you. It is a path of possibilities, where there is no traced path but formed by your footsteps - a state where you are not limited to something, embracing all opportunities.

When you allow yourself to connect fully, you become available to higher vibrational frequencies that want to communicate with you. Validation is a gift to oneself, and this gift already exists within; you have to discover it and consciously accept it.

You embody the universe's wisdom, so allow this wisdom to run through you now. Give yourself all the gifts you want to receive and be a blessing to others. Life is a sacred ceremony, and your commitment is to be in a perpetual state of celebration. Make your intention to experience joy and give unconditionally, understand that giving is receiving, and become worthy of everything by giving. Become the source of all that you aspire to manifest in your life. Stand in confidence and affirmation.
Remember who you are!

Breathing Consciously

Breathing is becoming aware of your truest essence,
and allows all your senses to show you the magic within.

There are numerous ways to anchor yourself in your true essence to facilitate the flow of information, but one of the most potent methods involves the practice of conscious breathing. Once, during a meditation session, I asked my higher self, "What is the first step in the process of going deep? How can I initiate a connection within?" The response was profound: "Connect to your breathing; it will set your journey in motion."

Connecting with one's breath holds immense significance, as it bridges the realms of Heaven and Earth. As an element, air acts as the link between the physical and the ethereal. So, breathe consciously to feel your essence and connect with the spiritual plane.

Matias De Estefano, author and spiritual teacher, described the word "Spiritual," as deriving from "Spirare" and "Spiritualis," the attribute of breath - the quality of breathing that gives us life. The breath of life awakens our being; the soul revives in the breath of the Spirit. Therefore, at a universal level, "Spirituality" is related to the respiratory system of the Universe - The Spirit is breath.

Breathe gently and feel the air entering your lungs, repeating the cycle throughout your meditation. Breathing is the main conduit for connecting with the universe; it is the most powerful tool to experience the cosmos. Allow this flow to take you places the mind cannot, And when your thoughts inevitably intrude, gently guide your focus back to your breath.

When approached with mindfulness, all breathing practices transform you into a clear channel for receiving information. Every breathing technique roots you deeply in your essence, guiding you back to the eternal moment of the here and now, essential for connecting to the cosmos - As above, so below.

During meditation, your breath becomes shallower, and at times, it may even seem to pause momentarily. Embrace this phenomenon; there is no need to deliberate on when to inhale again. Trust your body's innate wisdom; it will initiate inhalation as required. During meditation, centering your attention on your breath harmonizes your body and mind, ushering you into the present moment with greater clarity. There is so much information in silence, breathing consciously, and being present.

Being Present

There is solely power in the now
I am forever here and forever now.

You are presently existing in the "now." Every event in the past was a "now" moment, and every event in the future will always be a "now" moment. Therefore, it's essential to be fully present and in touch with your essence during meditation to access and engage with universal wisdom.

All forms of channeling and connecting manifest in the present moment; they do not reside in the future. The information you wish to receive is available to you now, whether you realize it or not.

While the connection has always been present, you can only establish it through your intent, as previously mentioned. Occasionally, it might seem like you are receiving guidance and information with a delay, but that only depends on your capacity to be completely present. The time it takes to establish a connection with higher frequencies depends on your ability to engage with and commit to the present moment fully. Do not expect the answer; the answer is always here and "now."

Contact with your higher self or higher vibrational beings occurs when you consciously connect with every aspect of existence. These beings are already here, whether angelic, cosmic, or of higher vibration. All you need to do is center yourself in your heart in "this moment" and feel, listen, and observe.

Higher frequency beings don't perceive linear time as we do. So when you call upon spirit guides, masters, and light beings, they show up; they don't negotiate whether they come or "not." And what you receive is always what you need to receive at this time, not later.

The "present" moment is a gift we experience with excitement, just like when we receive a present. This excitement will propel "instantly" a course of events that will allow you to become aware of the oneness you are with every frequency in the universe.

In being present in your heart, you find answers and not somewhere outside of you in the future. It is all happening instantly; create your reality by acknowledging this moment. Simplify your process by focusing on the here, the now, and nothing else. The moment you wait for the connection, you'll continue waiting until you realize that "You are the connection - here and now."

The Retrieved Information

When you're fully present and ready to access what belongs to you, the information you want to retrieve will present organically and expansively.

The information you receive must be organic and expansive. By being organic, we mean recognizing that you are the natural source of information. You cannot force a connection or have expectations on how it will happen; this is why we stress the organic part. The more you feel comfortable getting to know and love yourself, the more these connections will happen organically, thus expanding your consciousness.

Expansion is infinite, and you're forever expanding; actually, the fact that you are reading this material is also part of that expansive path you are on. The channeled information you retrieve organically comes and expands in different ways, but mainly, the information downloads through emotions. Emotions are energy waves; all data moves through energy, and all emotions are energy.

Feeling positive is crucial before channeling, as the resulting connection mirrors your emotional and mental state. Contact may occur in many ways, such as telepathy, emotions, visualizations, speech, auditory perception, writing, singing, and even physical expressions like dance and mudras. When you completely let go and embrace surrender, you can interpret the message in many ways that will be unique to you.

A friend once told me, "I wish I could channel information as you do." It is imperative to avoid comparing your process to anyone else's; you always receive the information the way that best suits your path. Surrender all expectations and allow the channeling to flow through you perfectly, the way only you can experience it.

Do you desire to connect, communicate, and receive guidance from high-frequency beings with love and clarity? Yet, do you extend the same loving and clear communication to those in your immediate circle? Is your interaction with others consistently infused with love and clarity, or does it occasionally stem from the egoic mind and lead to confusion?

It's essential to recognize that our interactions with others mirror the information we receive. Therefore, when aiming to connect with higher frequency beings, be conscious of your communication style towards everyone, maintaining a loving and transparent approach. This way, you'll cultivate consistent communication across all levels of existence.

Observation Non Resistance & Fulfillment

Observation of the self is a way to become self-aware. Connecting with your emotions without resistance is very powerful because it gives you a sense of fulfillment.

Observing ourselves allows us to become mindful of our emotions, thoughts, and physical sensations, fostering a deeper understanding of our being. It encourages us to avoid judging ourselves, creating an environment to connect with our inner state. Recognizing our current emotional state is crucial, providing valuable insight into our inner landscape. Moreover, it prompts us to contemplate how we desire to feel during our journey of self-realization.

In this process of self-observation, we can uncover the beauty within ourselves, acknowledging our essential nature and expressing gratitude for the blessings that define us. Embracing this gratitude leads to a state of "Non-Resistance," where we release the burden of pressure, doubt, and self-judgment. Even when doubt emerges, it's an opportunity to sit with that feeling, accepting and finding peace. Fear-based emotions are transmuted into love as long as you make peace with them and commit to elevating your frequencies, often through connecting with gratitude, joy, or other high-vibrational emotions.

It's important to honor and acknowledge every emotion we experience, maintaining a sense of gratitude and making peace with our thoughts and any negative aspects that may arise. Confronting these negative aspects is a vital step toward non-resistance, a prerequisite for channeling higher vibrational beings.

The act of non-resistance towards our inner selves aligns with our original intention to connect with our heart center. This connection, in turn, facilitates interactions with other heart-centered beings, revealing a greater sense of unity and interconnectedness.

Fulfillment isn't the conclusion of our journey but rather the initiation of a new relationship with ourselves and the boundless beings intrinsically connected with us. It's the realization that we are complete and that the connections we seek are merely pathways to further our understanding of the eternal wisdom within us. The journey of channeling involves self-discovery, allowing us to comprehend higher vibrational beings as we integrate various aspects of ourselves through a loving connection.

Questioning & Doubting

Questioning = Allowing
Doubting = Resisting

When you ask yourself, "Am I an open channel for universal wisdom?" Some individuals sense a firm affirmation within, entering a state of openness and allowance. However, when you doubt that this wisdom already resides within you, you deny your nature, resisting the information from flowing through you effortlessly.

Questioning is essential and valid during connection because it helps you understand your intentions and "whys." We consistently urge individuals to engage in self-inquiry because it leads to profound understanding. The correct answers unveil themselves when you pose the right questions. Moreover, self-questioning facilitates the birth of new possibilities in your life.

When you doubt your ability to connect and channel during this process, it signifies a lack of trust in your intuitive guidance. Therefore, eliminate all room for doubt during this process, as it is the most crucial aspect of your journey. While other elements may adapt to your distinctive approach, "self-doubt" is non-negotiable.

Embrace confidence, no matter how irrelevant the channeled information may appear initially. The guidance you receive always delivers a relevant message to your process. Trust the unfolding: the "visions, sensations, and sounds," assuming the role of a neutral observer, free from judgment.

You can ask for guidance during your journey, so be very specific. For example, ask questions like: "What's the next step I need to take for my next level of spiritual evolution?" or "What can I do....(in a particular scenario) that is for my highest good and the highest good of all?".

Asking questions is one of many ways you will receive that answer. You can also set the intention to receive the information you need the most at any given moment. You'll be amazed at how relevant the information you get is, bringing much-needed clarity.

Additionally, if you already have the answer to something you have asked before but want "confirmation," feel free to ask for a natural and undeniable sign in material form. Subsequently, you'll manifest individuals or circumstances that will provide the confirmation you request.

The Process

It's not about enjoying the process;
it's about you enjoying yourself.
The process doesn't have emotions; you do.
You don't trust the process; you trust yourself.
You are the process.

The process is the journey you must go through to reach the point you have traced for yourself. It is an inner path that takes you through places that already exist but that you have yet to experience. Everything you want to manifest in your reality already exists, but there is a belief that you have to create it. So, based on your frequency level, you align with what has always been there through the process.

The process is limited to your understanding of how long or short it should be, how hard or how easy it will unfold. The simpler you make this process, the more fun it will be. It doesn't have to be complex or complicated since it is in your innate. The more you think it's intricate and complex, the more it shall be that way.

This connection process is about expansion; the key opens doors and builds the path. Although you're always connected, your mind usually only justifies connecting to higher vibrational frequencies with these steps. As you get more comfortable in your practice, you'll also realize the process/time to channel starts to shorten.

We invite you to dedicate some time to connect with yourself during this process; you will find this practice gratifying by learning to crave consciously and cherish getting in touch with yourself every day. You'll find a beautiful moment of intimacy in every journey that no one else can give you. This time of aloneness with you will always offer a message attached with a lesson or a realization.

Your process is a personal choice, and only you can dictate that; no one can decide your process as it is as unique as life itself. Learn to enjoy and love yourself; that will reflect how your process will manifest because as you feel, your process shall be.

You are neither made nor defined by the process; create the process how you decide because it matters. The path you experience starts with each step you take. Remember that there is no rush to get anywhere because you're already there. Surrender to your process, not to where you want to go. The destination already exists, and you create the process with every step. Just like the energy of Master Jesus once said during meditation:
"The work has been done; now you just have to go through the process."

Connecting to your Heart

As you focus on self-expansion, the entire landscape of possibilities expands along.

We've provided suggestions, from adopting a lighter diet to cultivating sacred space and harnessing the power of setting your intentions. Naturally, these are adaptable variables; you can tailor them to your unique approach for a more organic experience. However, a fundamental element crucial to enhancing your connection beautifully is "Connecting to your Heart."

This connection holds the utmost significance, enabling you to engage and interact with higher realms of existence. Connecting to your heart is similar to having your "WI-FI" - the energy source facilitating channeling. It involves cherishing yourself above all connections, whether with guides, masters, or anything else. Recognizing that you're one with everything, you are both the guidance and the master you've been searching for.

But how does one forge this connection? Once again, there's no wrong way to do this, so we'll share what works for us. In our understanding, a "conscious connection to the heart" is a state of self-love and gratitude towards oneself. Deep contact with your heart starts with aligning and being grateful for every aspect of your being (positive and negative equally). It is the recognition of the entirety and wholeness of the divine within you without excluding or judging the negative ones.

Connecting to the heart involves acknowledging that you embody all possibilities and potentialities; it's a sensation and a recollection of your true self. While you constantly "remember and never forget," you can occasionally become distracted and shift your focus away from the heart. To connect with your core, you can use visualization to guide you as you venture into your heart and explore its depths. Dive within deeply; you'll find joy in the manifested emotions, visions, and sensations.

Connecting to your heart lies in recognizing your potential to be all you can be. It's an acknowledgment of the highest, most sacred aspect of yourself. At that moment, other divine interactions can arise from the intention to feel your heart's guidance.

Close your eyes and spend time with yourself simply because you love being in your presence, without any expectations other than discovering your true self and making yourself the center of your attention. And at that moment, you've established a profound connection to your heart.

The Meditation

Throughout every chapter of this book, we have mentioned all aspects of what your meditation should ideally have. However, there are no formulas for meditating and reaching higher levels of awareness. All the pointers we have shared in previous chapters of this book will give you a general understanding of how to meditate to access inner guidance. Nevertheless, we encourage you to take charge of your process and create your unique way of channeling and connecting to higher vibrational frequencies, cosmic beings, and angelic energies.

"It is all within you & There is no wrong way to do it."

With this said, we will get you started with a few essential elements so you can be on your way back to your heart center. Are you ready to do this? Let's do it!

Sit comfortably in your sacred space; we recommend sitting on a lotus position representing the Merkabah shape (image 1). This sitting position will support your process, so make sure your back is straight; energy flows better when your back is aligned. You can lean against a wall if you like. Never compromise your comfort, so feel free to move your body anytime.

Now that you're comfortably seated, stretch your body. "move your head from side to side, release any tension from you neck and back." Make yourself yawn; yawning allows you to release the energy you no longer need.

Image 1

Connection to Gratitude

Close your eyes and focus on your breath; inhale and exhale naturally through the nose and start connecting to high vibrational emotions. Connecting to what makes you feel grateful, like family members, your children, pets, situations, and things that bring you happiness is vital. Draw a smile on your face; this signals your brain that good things are happening inside you, so you start secreting Serotonin and Oxytocin, modulating your mood and positive feelings.

Also, feel grateful for people or events that "don't feel good," because they are too part of your process. Make peace with anything that is bothering you at this time. Everything in your life is a blessing and a stepping stone that allows you to become the person you are today, and that is also a reason to be grateful. Connecting to gratitude raises your frequency, as gratitude is the highest vibrational emotion on Planet Earth.

Connection to Earth

At this moment, start to feel the Earth beneath you. Visualize thick roots growing from the bottom of your feet and toes and send them to the center of the Earth. See and feel your energy roots connecting to a bright white source of energy (the Heart of Mother Gaia).

On your next deep breath, inhale love from the heart of Gaia and feel the white source going up through your roots. Now, see it entering your feet, going up your legs, waist, lower abdomen, and back. The energy keeps moving up your chest, upper back, shoulders, and arms. - Next, visualize all the love of Gaia, "white energy" coming out from the palms of your hands. Lastly, feel the energy going through your neck and face and coming from the top of your head to the universe. You're now grounded and ready to fly while anchored to Mother Earth.
Say: I am Earth.

Connection to Air

Keep breathing slowly and become grateful for the Air entering your body; feel your lungs and appreciate this life source inside you. Remember that Air is the portal between the Etheric and the Physical. So breathe with intention and focus on constantly breathing during your entire meditation.
Say: I am Air.

Connection to Water

Bring your attention to your saliva and feel the water inside you. Connect to the tears you've cried and the sweat you've endured to become the beautiful person you are today. Feel your blood running through your veins, and be grateful for the life that provides to you.
Say: I am Water.

Connection to Fire

Picture your heart center as a ball of fire, and place your hands on your chest. Connect with your heartbeat and harmonize with the universe's rhythm (become one with the cosmos). Feel the fire within you burning and expanding throughout your body, transmuting any low vibrational energy you no longer need. As you see these energies transmuting, bless them and thank them for their service with love, compassion, and forgiveness.
Say: I am Fire.

Visualization

At this time, you will visualize a tetrahedron coming up from the center of the Earth inside your body through your Root chakra. Now picture a tetrahedron from heaven entering your Crown chakra (See Image 2).

Image 2

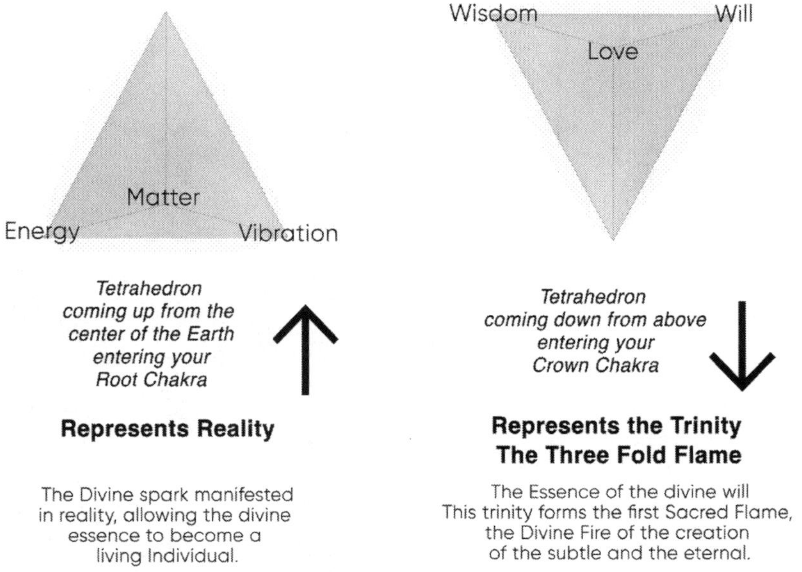

Left tetrahedron (pointing up): Matter, Energy, Vibration

Right tetrahedron (pointing down): Wisdom, Will, Love

Tetrahedron coming up from the center of the Earth entering your Root Chakra ↑

Tetrahedron coming down from above entering your Crown Chakra ↓

Represents Reality

The Divine spark manifested in reality, allowing the divine essence to become a living Individual.

**Represents the Trinity
The Three Fold Flame**

The Essence of the divine will
This trinity forms the first Sacred Flame, the Divine Fire of the creation of the subtle and the eternal.

Once both triangles have connected in the middle, see yourself inside, sitting on a lotus position, with the Merkabah lighting up and the tetrahedrons spinning in opposite directions.

Image 3

Following, bring your attention to a point between your eyes (third eye). Visualize yourself and the Merkaba in the middle of your eyes; with intention and practice, this exercise will allow you to see every dimension beyond this reality. You don't have to focus on it too much; just become aware that the Merkabah is on your forehead. However, whenever you feel distracted, bring your awareness back to that point.

Image 4

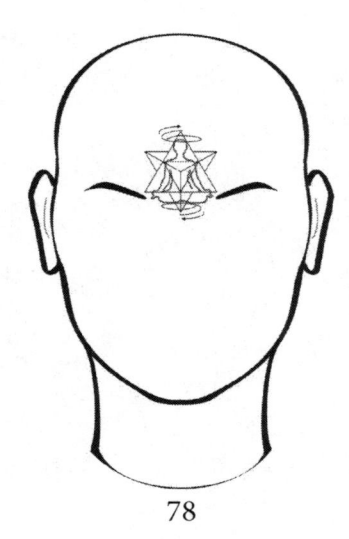

The Prayer: Now, allow yourself to access universal wisdom and become a clear channel for high vibrational frequencies to express themselves through you. Feel happy, validated, empowered, one with the universe, and say:

I, "your full name," lovingly give myself permission to access and interact with my "Akashic Records. So I can consciously connect with my heart, my higher aspects, the wisdom of the cosmos, and the highest frequencies of the universe "here and now." May this connection and channeling session be for my highest purpose and the guidance that best suits my process "here and now." You can add any intention "you desire" to your prayer; make sure it's always for your highest good and the highest good of all people around you.

You are "now" sending a powerful message to the higher consciousness, so feel the connection. Your intention carries a vibrational frequency that serves as a mechanism to access the infinite wisdom that you are.

Visualization: Visualize your body sitting where you are as if watching yourself from above. That brings you into being fully present.

- Place your hands in a praying position in front of your chest. This mudra creates a conscious connection to your heart center. It represents the union between heaven and Earth.

- And now, create a triangle shape with your hands in front of your chest. This pyramidal shape opens a window from your heart to a multidimensional portal.

- Extend your arms and allow the portal (triangle shape) to open. Now, wait for an inner voice to say, "The portal is now open." You can also make this statement and affirm your desires.

- Become aware once again of the Merkabah in front of your third eye. See yourself traveling in your Merkabah from your third eye through the opened portal (hands in a triangle shape).

- Once again, bring your hands to your heart in a praying position as a sign of oneness. And lastly, place your hands on your chest "left on top of the right" as a sign of gratitude for this connection.

Keep your awareness of the Merkabah in the middle of your eyes, and keep the intention of being present. Surrender to the here and now. Don't wait for any response at any specific moment. Instead, be grateful you are dedicating time to yourself and making your primary intention to feel good. Feeling good will expedite the information to come through and happen faster.

Be patient; the message and the connection are already there. You have to raise your frequency by genuinely surrendering to the present moment so you can tune into it. Know that the information can come through in different ways. You can see images and geometry, listen to an inner voice, feel a presence, or have a deep understanding and realization.

From now on, it is you and your heart, so - Breathe - Surrender and Allow.

You are here for the experience - Feel
You are here for the inner guidance - Listen
You are here for you - Connect.

Adonai.

Commitment & Consistency

Meditation is just like any other skill in life, and it is all about your ability to commit to this practice. Remember that it is a practice of Self-Love and Self-Realization, but it takes time to master it. This process of connecting and channeling is a skill we have developed throughout many years of constant practice and commitment to ourselves and serving others.

Commitment is different from consistency. Commitment is a quality towards yourself, but how consistent you are is how often you practice that to which you are committed. You can meditate once a month or once a week; that depends on your commitment to this practice. Combining your level of dedication and consistency determines the outcome you will experience.

It was vital never to compare our channeling and connecting process with anyone else's. Like many people wanting to learn to channel, we were also looking for the same information many years ago. So when we started our awakening, we consistently read books to learn how everyone else did it. While that was very useful, we understood that we could only connect and channel uniquely and at our own pace.

When you connect to your heart, you will connect to that energy suitable to communicate with you. It doesn't matter whether it is galactic or angelic; it doesn't matter; there is always an aspect of you present and available. And the perfect message will come through.

You are the connection and the answer you're searching for elsewhere. So, no matter what meditation you practice to experience the contact, know that you are already there. Remember that there is a beautiful and unique way to connect and access the information you wish to receive.

It is all within you, and there is no wrong way to do it.

Remembering the Warrior

The warrior goes in silence, feels the body, and observes emotions.

The warrior's way is to walk in silence without any distractions, aiming for excellence and stepping into greatness, excited to be here and back to the basics. The warrior walks with humility, always wanting to learn like a good student but knowing about inner mastery. Hopeful but sure, never doubtful but constantly questioning - "Is it possible?" The answer is always yes.

Keep wondering.
Keep living your dreams awake!

You are all going through a spiral ascension process, and developing your way to connect with high vibrational beings will be unique. No one can teach you how to access the wisdom within you. The connection and guidance you're looking for are YOU!

Mantra:
I AM the message and the messenger.
I Am the guide and the guidance.
I Am the answer to all my questions.
I AM - YOU.